THE GRAMMAR OF WITCHCRAFT

By
David Parry M.A.

Copyright © David Parry and Mandrake of Oxford, 09

First edition
All rights reserved. No part of this work may be reproduced or utilized in any form by any means electronic or mechanical, including *xerography, photocopying, microfilm*, and *recording*, or by any information storage system without permission in writing from the author.

Published by
Mandrake of Oxford
PO Box 250
OXFORD
OX1 1AP (UK)

Also by David Parry and available from Mandrake

Caliban's Redemption

A CIP catalogue record for this book is available from the British Library and the US Library of Congress.

Contents

Our Rite of Passage
or *hearing* those secret harmonies ———————————— 5

Prefatory Acknowledgements
To A Heathen Readership ———————————— 11

1. Wishbones And Weasels. ———————————— 14

2. A Dialogue Between Crows ———————————— 20

3. Prophylactic Signs ———————————— 28

4. His Green Italian Owl ———————————— 38

5. High Brooms ———————————— 47

6. Questioning Tate Britain ———————————— 55

7. Lord Heimdall's Revealing ———————————— 62

A Postscript Of Valentines ———————————— 70

Selective Glossary ———————————— 87

Our Rite of Passage or *hearing* those secret harmonies

The Grammar of Witchcraft is an epic mirror for Albion today and a unique and complex treatise for universal witchery, tapping into the most fertile wellsprings of our unsettled culture, through the deeply familiar and beloved, impish, prophetic and sensitive eyes and resolute voice of Caliban; with a voice as old as time for sure - who unveils this love poem to the sacred 'always' of our language, a figure bent and cultivated with experience, bitter with foresight and the precision of his atavistic and intellectual objectivity. Caliban - out of his introspective skin now, self-sent out into the world now, a learned magical imperfect pylon, crackling with the bounty of secret lore and due respect and love for it - seeks to speak with a precious humanity and seer-like forthrightness, throwing down the gauntlet of a unique cultural plea, to understand every aspect of what unites and what tears us apart. This work does not merely illuminate the prismatic power of witchery, it demonstrates it completely; language as power and power through language. Language as breath.

Not since Derek Jarman's guerrilla masterpiece "Jubilee", with its subtle cultural time-slips, back in 1977, has the bristling, tortured, neglected and yet fecund power of cultural and lexical identity, of society and spirit, been so beautifully examined and realised. Caliban is a true voice of edgy philosophical reason and reminds us of what powers of the psyche and elementalism we have lost or are fast losing through our fingers like the finest sand. Caliban's skrying stone within, like that of Dr Dee, provides us with the stimulus, the learning, the energetic key. Like a true elementary grammar where every word has its symbolic station, this work is a treasure house of learning - to unfold, unpick, respect, explore and worship as its doors open and close with their illumination and our shame, at what has been lost.

Original magical texts are rare and deeply occult things, to be sure; occult in the true sense of secret things and the unveiling and experiencing of secret things and the deceptive logic of surface and the in-between. It is down to the defined and attuned human perception to pick them up - to attend with joy, the ecumenical rite of pagan worship that this subtle work extends to the reader, or should I say beloved neophyte. The poems throughout the *Grammar*, like gossamer, so delicately woven, so aptly described by Caliban, as Valentines, are very old in voice and so precisely created as pure love; they exert an influence that leads us into the philosophy and arguments of light and shade, of spiritism and the ever-present urban consciousness that none can escape, save through pockets of captive remembrance, batteries of resonant occult power. For this is such a work - with its roots in the architecture of knowledge.

Caliban articulates the essence of witchery - the living, breathing ancient sense of it, and the notion that language and identity, personal, cultural and ethnic are the inextricably linked strands of DNA that waver, subsumed, unspoken, misunderstood, beaten and shunned. It is Caliban's bold journey - our own defender of heathen faith - thee faith, if you will - embraced, assaulted and embraced again by the fecundity of thought and argument and dialectic - that is so precious and which provides the framework for his unexpected questions and those that assail him. What is spirit? What is consciousness and philosophy? What is identity, ethnicity and what is the concept of land? Who is brave and formidable enough to ask or take on such questions but Caliban, in our current landscape, exposing his mettle to ectoplasmic concourse and to raw philosophy and voices from the very source of things? Who is brave enough to put himself - the "oh lucky man" of our time, into a journey of discovery and revelation and spiritual tuning and deconstruction, determining to return to London to practice his own supranatural contemporaneous assault on the establishment, the brittle, vulnerable, empty shells that haunt our culture as one-dimensional abstract sadnesses ...this young Blake-Boy, himself walking with flames of glory and of experience. Would that dear Derek Jarman - poet of the eye - were here still to film Caliban's assault on the Tate.

Caliban is a true priest and practices what he preaches, self-initiated; a literary and esoteric witch of the highest order - closing down the ritual power of his work, delivering the most eloquent and subtle postscript to this work, a veritable Valentine of the deepest sensitivity and worship, beyond sexuality and into highest humanity, defining and redefining our relationship to the 'everness' of the Goddess and the secret nature that is the joy of life. Caliban takes it further though, with a cultural constancy that the literary establishment is too frigid and afraid to embrace.. "I recognise aspects of our Goddess everywhere, but perhaps particularly in *my own people* and when I notice in them another poet, he or she becomes my own true valentine". In his many encounters along the way, that will surprise and delight the willing neophyte, a deeply spiritual pagan sensibility and belief - innocence and experience - unfolds as symbolic as it is possible to be; like Masonic marks in curb stones, trampish cuts upon a tree or the tears of the palest moon that haunts - they seep into our tortured indiscriminate folk memory and confusion from out the fevered generosity of his soul. To walk abroad in Lud and up the backbone of Modern Albion, radiating revelation is a lonely but exalted path. Caliban treads this path with sacred purpose and with an eye to understanding the pain of it. Bitter pain that leads to revelation and beloved acceptance of truth and beauty.

Caliban fertilises sensibility and language herself, deflowers any notion of complacency and protects and honours that distinction between those who have the perception and the spirit to be initiated and those who do not. This magical grammar is a door to initiation - *is* initiation. Like the text of *Caliban's Redemption*, it is a bastard stripe across the back - raw root - politics, raw philosophy, sexual and spiritual defiance in a oak-carven grail for the Goddess. Caliban's esoteric rite of passage is pre-destined - it has to happen, more for us than for him and the precious and genuine deeply poetic insistency of his voice - the central timbre and spirit of this work - resonates with the authenticity of the radical, of the timeless minstrel rhymer, of the philosopher bent poet escaped from his island, of the wise woman leaning upon a gate staring beyond what she sees into infinity and blazing runic nebulas. Caliban has dreamed and lived a vision that goes beyond our understanding and Caliban unfolds it as a true visionary, for us to thus understand and drink deeply of! Bold statements abound, but these are bold statements forged in the furnace of pure spirit - the sub-atomic current where truth and beauty reside in their earliest and oldest form as *ONE*.

This rite of passage is religious and rightly full of revelation and as you journey through the humanity and generous consciousness of Caliban, from Liverpool and back to London, think on this pilgrim's sojourn and his oral history and paean; this subtle burning testament of Caliban redeemed, articulator of the truly Heathen timeless lexicography of true lore. In every single word you read of the *Grammar*, by the turn of every page shall you feel the power of change, the bristling elemental breeze of purest Witchery, for the written word of old that comes anew doth mark the soul.

Jonathan Wood
Copyright 2009

Prefatory Acknowledgements To A Heathen Readership

It is with a certain sense of trepidation that I begin this opening comment, since so many dear friends have helped me to write these Mythopoetic scenarios and verses. Some have already passed into Valhallah and are so illustrious that I scarcely dare to mention them, although it is impossible to compose modern English letters without their influence. My debt to these ancestors is overwhelming, which is why I name their names while genuflecting in due reverence to; Christopher Marlowe, Charles Dickens and Ted Hughes, being ever mindful of their pre-eminence. Others are Spiritists, and despite being as illustrious in their own way are less formidable for that very reason. I include Assagioli and Dr. Roger Evans, along with the incomparable Maxine Sanders. Still other friends have helped me with their expertise, patience and proof reading abilities. They include Sanan Aliyev without whose loyal friendship life in London would be grimly depleted, Katon Shual, Dr. Karina Halstead, Tony Gulvin, the Reverend Presley Sutherland along with his husband David Bedella and lastly, Master of the strict observance Ms. Jacqueline Hackett.

I have no further opening remarks to make accept that "High Brooms", "Questioning Tate Britain" and "Lord Heimdall's Unfolding" were originally published in foetal form as articles in *Psychic World*. Additionally, the poems "Caliban in Clover", "The Pilgrim" as well as "Blake's Resurgence" were first published in the 6th edition of the occasional literary journal *Through The Woods*. Thus clearly demonstrating that the *Grammar of Witchcraft* is a key to the *Universitas Litterarum*; a mysterious poetic mechanism allowing us to unlock the textual mysteries of the Pleroma Itself. Blessed be Jesse Thompson, wherever you are.

Decays flavour confounds every reason,

Either confuses or confounds

In the Inferno of forgotten lies,

Where sinister airs under All-Good Spirit

Sow discord disguised as dissent.

Between natural neighbours, between books,

Between innocent souls in Midsummer grief

First crushed and quelled by sad circumstance

Then pugnaciously cast in dystopian scenes

Which arena each fist as a victims defence:

As a bloodstained cousin to the thunder,

And rival to the reddening earth

Yet forgetful that in the Enormity of Being

Hidden glories still dwarf each tragic event

With bright transcendent Light, with Sound,

With tribal regeneration,

And with drying dust and frozen ashes

Under our icy northern footfalls.

Wishbones and Weasels.

Spirits are like numbers. They are both in nature and above nature. English witches have known this since the time of Good King Bladud. It was the type of unnerving knowledge that kept us constitutionally separated from the heavily industrialised cities. Separate and close to the forests. Apart that is from the city of Liverpool where nearly everything seems visceral. Even the overpoweringly Christian architecture embodies a rare and richly dynamic quality. Perhaps that's why entering Liverpool always feels like a threshold experience.

For Caliban this city continually held unexpected initiations. On this occasion he had been invited to a lesbian wedding because of his apparently ironic belief that love and sex were antithetical. Strangely enough the happy couple thought he had a point. But at that precise moment in time it didn't really matter. He was early. Hours early as usual, and the wrong side of the river Mersey. From where he stood he could see the Liver-birds glinting in the sky like phoenix twins already aflame with regeneration. Burning and aflame. That's why they personified a community which still had all the restless tactile energy of adolescent libido; even after all these centuries. It was then, with a similar sense of energised frustration that Caliban passed an hour or two by walking along the rivers embankment, trying to find a bench to sit on and orientate himself. Possibly this was the entire problem, apart from his fucking hang-over. His gaydar needed a sense of provincial perspective.

As if by coincidence, he noticed a Scouse Mother and young Daughter also looking for a seat. "Christ!", they were a sight more than a vision. Mother Scouse was as pale as unused parchment. Little light lingered in her weary eyes. She looked old, decades before her dotage and was physically bent double like Shakespeare's archetypal crone Hecate. It was as though her own body was trying to finally break the years of bad fortune in two, like a dry forgotten wishbone. Brittle dirty hair protruded from her head, similar in colour to the tethered twigs of a bisom broom and with roughly the same texture. From a distance it looked as though evil forces nestled there, although unsettled and twisting in their surly incarceration. Once they would have been called "pixie locks" and treated with a slight revulsion. Nowadays it just seemed unfashionable. These powers took their revenge, however, by making Mother Scouse's legs puffy with oedema, grotesquely contrasting with her spindly upper half. To cap it all, she wore a faded football scarf around her neck smelling of rancid defeat.

Her Daughter, on the other hand, was immaculate; a fairy creature from a nursery-rhyme world. Not a single speck of dust settled on her. She was clean, sallow skinned, blue-eyed and with hair like reddening autumn leaves. Caliban wasn't certain whether it was a case of gentrification or parental projection. "Coooohhh!" He heard the girl begging her Mother to feed the single bedraggled pigeon nearby, so after finding a corporation bench to sit on, they threw some bread at the ground to attract the birds' balding attention. Almost out of nowhere a flock of plump, moth-eaten pigeons were soon staggering in their direction. The girl gurgled with delight and threw some more bread at the ground. Then she noticed that one of the pigeons had very distinctive markings and stood out among the rest:

"Look mummy, that one's ugly and not like the others. It's different."

The young Mother peered over.

"That's the evil one. Be careful. Run away quickly."

The girl squealed with mock horror and ran back to the false comforts of her Mother. Caliban was stunned at the remark and stared at them. They didn't notice! He suddenly realised that this was one of the ways in which crippling intolerance was passed on by morally bankrupt parents from one generation to the next. Their own unresolved bile unconsciously expressed in ways that were bound to blind the next generation to compassion. After all, ignorance could be transmitted as well as wisdom, under the guise of kisses and cuddles. Mother Scouse wanted someone to be on her side. Anyone really! She wanted life to be fair, but had never thought about its intrinsic inhumanity. Perhaps he should say something? Caliban looked in their direction, but it was already too late. Daughter Scouse had tired of pigeons and so, collecting themselves, they waddled further down the river side.

Being different has always been considered evil. Caliban knew that natural witches have had to endure this thoughtless prejudice for centuries. As homosexuals and lesbians, we were seen as sexual deviants, even though everything that made us alien to Christendom gave us power. In a sense, our sexuality offered an unspoken challenge to the repressed communities surrounding us, while saving us from the self-contempt plaguing our neighbours. They were like the bushes of a poorly planted hedgerow, whose roots vengefully strangled and painfully suffocated each other in a desperate fight for survival. Their branches haunted by back biting weasels and bickering bats, ready to astrally scratch and claw anyone who disturbed them. Every now and again their inherited anxieties oozed out the poisonous sap of persecution. First it tainted the Jews, then us, finally staining their own speculative books. But our Magic protected us from the domestic vacuity stifling their unpleasantly intertwined lives. Our very strangeness insulated us from the inauthenticity that mutilated their pleasures. We had distinctive rules about gender equality, cleanliness and food, which told us their groundless ways would lead to madness. As witches, we insisted that placing solar consciousness on a pedestal above nature necessarily led to a radical disrespect for the Greater-Family-of-Life, and we have been proved right. The Church Fathers ignored our warnings at their peril. Centuries ago, Sir Francis Bacon rebelled against them to save our Hearth from further threat, and in the due course of time Charles Darwin himself took up our hylozoists torch. We adapted, while their insincere world was only postponing its inevitable decay.

Musing on this ancestral paradox, Caliban wondered why it seemed that everyone these days thought they were different. Maybe particularly in Liverpool. In reality they were only different like everyone else. Another irony! To add insult to injury, if someone was actually different, in the sense of kind-hearted, or generous, like his lesbian friends, their distinctiveness somehow overshadowed the light of their virtue to the people around them. "Oh, sweet Jesus", his head wouldn't stop pounding as though a Scots military band in full procession was marching through his brain. He felt vaguely nauseous. Fuck this hang-over and fuck history, he needed to find the girls and get a hair-of-the-dog at this fucking wedding.

"Beware the werewolf and his ways",

Once said a woodsman's wife,

"For poppy seeds flower between his teeth

When the Moon shines weird and white.

And once bitten by this loathsome beast

Only madness enflames the mind

As his poetry sings in blood possessed

By the rhythm of Romantic rhyme.

By the rhythm of Romantic rhyme, my dear,

By the rhythm of Romantic rhyme,

Only lunacy crowns a belligerent brow

With the rhythm of romantic rhyme".

So as the Sunshine lights the day

Give thanks to bright heaven above

That another cold night has passed away

Without the werewolf falling in love.

A Dialogue Between Crows

The same-sex Service was to be held at St. Breeders; a third irony. As a guest from out of town, Caliban had been given a highly detailed map and advised to get a cab. He was meant to be looking for the only Methodist church feeling magnanimous enough to "officially" celebrate this type of union. For fucks sake! This made no sense to him at all, since the idea behind every type of marriage seemed rather similar. Change necessitates choice. No matter what sexual orientation a person had, getting a partner implied that everything in life would be different and doubled. It was an undeserved blessing as well as a crippling curse. In some mystical sense the couple became part of a single uncoordinated whole, which is inevitably more than the sum of its individual parts. Years previously he had read that as a man and woman make love they become an angel. No doubt! But, gay lovers in particular bond closely on a subtle, physical, level. From experience Caliban knew when two tough male bodies held each other down, they form a clenched demi-god: a man greater than Hercules could ever be on his own. As men they locked themselves into a four armed, four legged miracle of flesh. Three girls therefore actively evolve into a twelve-limbed-love-Goddess.

His cabby had never heard of the church, or at least said he hadn't, so Caliban kept reading the map despite his directional sense always being crap under pressure. Anxiously, he looked out of a dirty window admiring the unexpectedly leafy suburbs as well as the opulent colours of the brickwork.

"I think we turn left at the next crossroads."

"What's that you said mate?"

"Left at the crossroads and then up the hill."

"Sorted. The clock is ticking away, tick, tick, tick". The cabby inadvertently twitched his ferret nose, wiping away a rivulet of drool with long, sticky, fingers.

"Cool".

Caliban hated saying "cool", along with the entire kitsch vocabulary surrounding emphatic expletives.

A tired old Crow with obsidian eyes suddenly flew across the road and hid somewhere above a parked Ford Fiesta. Just out of sight, feathers then frantically flapped with all the semblance and the seeming of an omen. Turning a corner, the cab drove closely towards the sound. Caliban saw a younger bird standing above the prostrate body of its older rival, plucking at the former's defeated plumage: an extremely bad esoteric correspondence. Every witch knows there are clearly times when signs and portents bubble up from the depths of existence. During the Glorious Revolution, we were painfully aware that some auguries could testify against us. Black Shuck the Demon Dog could speak Gospel Truth when it suited him, although consensus held Norfolk Cats of every colour would hold their tongues. Witches such as Agnes Waterhouse also claimed that consorting with Toads proved equally reliable. She noted these creatures would often become Familiar Imps, or in other words, forbidden, bestial lovers. Indeed, before her hanging, the pleasure she received from these "love-pygmies" had become almost legendary.

Caliban's familiar was a monkey. His name was Mike. The Almanacs warn witches against monkeys, but they had been instantly attracted to each other. Mike was a huge muscular boy, six foot three inches tall, hazel-eyed and really hairy. He wore tight Khaki shorts to show off his butt, complimented by a white tank top. There was a heated chemistry between them from the beginning, despite the obvious fact that the monkey was afraid of him. Like every other witch, Caliban suckled one of these Imps. He fed him through a supernumerary nipple marking the dwarf's genetic superiority over heterosexuals. In the past, our enemies would search for hidden teats all over our bodies with their prying, sensual hands. They tended to claim these unnatural protuberances were completely insensitive to pain and incapable of bleeding, shortly before torturing us. Perhaps nothing really changes.

As Caliban sat in the back seat looking for local landmarks, he noticed the shadow of Matthew Hopkins and the shade of Charles Fort sitting opposite him, arguing about Oracles and Imps. From beneath his wide-rimmed hat, the lean and looming Witchfinder General was horrified by these happenings. He stroked his long grey nose, and he muttered under his thin breath:

"Phenomenology or Witchcraft, I, Sir see not the difference. You like these bizarre and monstrous events because you be a limb of Satan yourself, Master Fort."

Glowing with a genial light, Fort's plump spirit shone with a greater luminosity than usual. He responded by saying, "Oh come, come, what Witchcraft? Creative Nature serenades us men at every moment. I have heard that in the forests of England, there have been times when stones were known to give Good Counsel and brooks have babbled with satirical comments. Chaucer must have heard this on his travels, as well as Ben Johnson when he trod the boards. Unlike the philosophers, these poets would let the planet speak to them personally, refusing to lecture the world about its essential processes. Far too few thinking men have ever had the genuine courage, or imaginative insight, to follow this lyrical path".

Hopkins tightened his grip on the cane he carried, wrinkling a heavy brow:

"Lyricism and laxity. I was the youngest member of the Puritan Commission and their rational instrument against the forces of Exotic Romanticism. The intellectual freedom you extol is but licence to grasp the ungodly. What does truth need to know of Omens or humour? Devil's work, Sir!"

Fort sagaciously felt his moustache and crooned, "How can the mystery of life be without laughter? We should delight in the flowering of Creativity, while rejecting any possible interpretation. Whose truth? First-hand experience is more valuable than third-hand explanation. The word 'unnatural' makes no sense. If something can happen in nature, it is then, natural!"

Caliban could no longer contain himself and grumbled:

"Neither of you understand witchcraft."

They both looked at him with surprise.

"Neither of you."

Before his unwelcome travelling companions could speak, Caliban continued:

"We worship the All-Seeing Eye of Mother Energy burning in the Messianic activities of Her Triangular Son, who constantly ascends back to His Mother. For us, He becomes Incarnational Flesh and Phenomena, tasting the knowledge that flesh alone knows. But He is still only Her Son. She is Sovereign: the Absolute 'I' observing Herself in created things. Historically our energic religion once communicated in the secret Mystery-cults of Eleusis, Corinth and Blessed Samothrace. When these centres of learning were suppressed our wisdom was taught in the poetic colleges of Iceland and Denmark."

"Can't hear you mate." The cabby looked confused.

"What?"

"I couldn't make out yer novelle directions. Don't ice my grill big belly man, I needs my props."

"Oh sorry, just talking to myself. Keep going."

"Sorted."

Both the Witchfinder and the Phenomenologist disappeared in a thunder-clap with an air of indignation.

"Bloody 'ell, strange weather, sounds like Jack Frost versus the Naked Chef oh-yeah? Hope Chef bitch-slapped his snowman and stuck the carrot up his fuckin' arse. Good job yer got this cab."

Caliban didn't say anything. He felt quiet and thoughtful, remembering that during the Persecution, we told the likes of Hopkins that our Craft offered a magical perspective we would defend with our lives because it burned with the immediacy of Her Being. Yet as a peculiar Gnosis, our understanding all but flickered out in the public domain at the end of the seventeenth century. We were tired of the turbulence, turning instead to indirect communication and Hollywood.

On balance however, Fort was closer to our faith, since he guessed nature's soul sent tokens to its lovers in weird, wonderful, ways. Caliban recalled as a child, seeing spectral balls of light in the night sky. They were crystal white in colour and seemed to be following him like expectant eyes overseeing his journeys. One Lammas-tide, he silently challenged one of these spheres to prove it was objective. Within moments, he was answered as the globe streaked ahead of him, leaving a brilliant trail behind it. A courting couple kissing in nearby trees shrieked with surprise as the Vision-Splendid vanished. Caliban, nonetheless, felt excited and frustrated. Her ways were indeed very hard to fathom.

"Ere wees are whack". The cab stopped at the entrance to an imposing grey stone building.

"I've only got a tenner."

"Sorted, me ole mate."

"Thanks".

Caliban wondered how many more times that guy would say "Sorted" in the next few hours. He got out and walked up to the church.

Only dark stars shine with loves real light

In modern Anglo-Saxon times

And only misfit minds descend to true insight

Beneath green sepulchral vines

For the Hellish depths in a human heart

Hold wonders more numerous than Heavens Immense

Or Asgarths Sacred Glory, or cold Nirvanic Bliss,

Or such a Soul as John Barleycorn

Who as a cereal being in nature's fertile design

Never knew the purgation of partial harvesting

Or the need to behave like Jesus

To be welcomed as the British Christ:

Himself crowned with once holy brambles

Above crusty, but still sacrificial brows

That bleed their now poisonous loams

Upon enigmatic fields reduced to a factory floor.

Prophylactic Signs

Caliban felt uncomfortable opening the cheerless Elm doors under the curiously judgemental stare of two elderly, fox-featured, clerics. Why were they stood there? Obviously, both clergymen knew he was gay and disliked his confident gait. The dwarf however was unperturbed, since he was deeply in debt to the shining Orisha Orun and a brother to his sunlight, so theoretically there should be no problem. Christianity was itself a Sun-Cult and early Christian Missionaries exhibited meticulous courtesy towards Sun Worshippers whenever they met them: irrespective of their sexuality. Nevertheless, he intuitively knew clerical ignorance, amplified over untold centuries of malice towards other spiritual paths, would allow no tolerance of him. Shit! He walked quickly passed them, nodding politely. There was also an usher at the entrance who rapidly guided him to his seat. "Ah yes, sir," she whispered, "You are with the bride's party". Caliban wondered how he could be with the "bride's party?" The words "husband" and "wife" have specific cultural connotations, and he didn't want to be anyone's husband or wife. Surely, gay and lesbian people didn't need to mimic the unsuccessful and largely mechanical customs of unhappy heterosexuals? Anyway, he thanked the burnished Heavens his pew was at the back.

To Caliban's surprise, more balding, fustian, clerics stood at the front alter. Then it hit him. Lesbians were trendy! If there was a better way to drag punters into church, he couldn't think of it. One of them was already intoning in a patronising voice: "As David so loved Jonathan and as Ruth so loved Naomi..." Caliban gasped, "Fuck, these people have no scruples." It seemed to him that one minute, homosexuals are excluded from full participation in the Church, and the next clerics are citing gay characters in the Bible. He took a prophylactic to lessen the tension. Only his planetary self had to suffer the hypocrisy surrounding him. Caliban relaxed, as the capsule began to loosen the silvery bonds between his various bodies. He had always known Witchcraft went further than the way of the Saints, because it invigorated all three vehicles, not just the fleshy physique. Orun once sang to him that the atom of soul grounded itself in the muddy soil of existence in an archetypal, imaginal and physical form: like a seed becoming a root, leaf and Lily flower - only to become a seed again. Orun enlighteningly chorused that when the cords were relaxed, each body could roam on its own plane, separately experiencing different parts of the one life uniting them. "A petal seeks light, a tendril needs darkness, but all is still a single plant," the monad stressed melodiously.

So for decades, Caliban obsessively studied the indentations of the physical body, finding himself intrigued by a range of divinatory techniques based on clinical observation concerning the marks and lines of the skin. Interpreting these engravings was traditionally known as Somatology, and methods included: Palmistry, Physiognomy, Neomancy and Phrenology. Until our Post-Modern period, such techniques signified peasant magic, despite the fact they decode the oldest talismans known to humanity. Maybe for this reason Caliban prized these tactile impressions, inscribing as they did, the semiotics of fate and the legacy of race memory.

His personal divinations always commenced with Palmistry (or to be more technical Chiromancy) since it uncovered primary psychological traits and unexpected future probabilities. Certainly, other witches followed similar procedures, yet in his practice Caliban concentrated on the lines of life, delightfully contouring the thumb, to tell his clients the length of time he or she had left to live. Caliban then focussed on the lines of the heart, to delve into the dominant emotions his client had already experienced, while discussing their passionate trajectories. Thirdly, Caliban pondered over the wrinkles on his client to calculate intellectual potential, warning him or her about personal excesses. Explanations followed, concerning issues raised by lines of health, along with ways to prevent any malady from manifesting. Lastly, he searched for lines of Destiny on the wrists of his clients, not only to prophesy achievements, but also to see if he was dealing with someone who may one day join the Teachers-Of-True-Epistemology.

Unlike inexperienced witches, Caliban knew this merely began a full sensual reading, since each finger has a symbolic attribution. He furthered his personal oracles by deciphering the finger nearest the thumb as the finger of King Jupiter, expressing Truest-Will. If it is naturally sculpted, this suggests a fondness for carousing, whereas a lengthy finger denotes the need to dominate others; accompanied by a lack of sensitivity towards basic human concerns. Next to this, is the finger of Old Father Saturn. A withered digit implies that the personality is unbalanced, whereas short joints reveal the intuitive psyche of a writer or painter. Afterward comes the finger of Radiant Apollo, or the ring finger. Any well-balanced person has a finely formed ring finger, but a stubby column indicates emotional dysfunction as well as restless introspection. Finally, there is the finger of Winged Mercury which if strong, suggests a seeker after sensual secrets, although if weak or twisted, screams of neuro-chemical disorders. Thumbs, like a silent dictionary, guide a witch over the fingers. They personify the libido itself. In which case, large turrets testify to a potent character, while a bent trunk betrays intrinsic melancholy. In situations of distress people often hide their thumbs, symbolising a desire to escape from the world.

The mounds are also extremely instructive. The mount of Sovereign Zeus relates to enthusiasm. If it is rudely coloured there is a tendency towards self-importance. Conversely a poorly shaped cushion shows a severe lack of confidence. Secondly, a well developed hill of Grandfather Cronus, whispers of a quiet disposition. Such a person is usually hard working with diligent predispositions towards their private affairs, although austerity taints their consciousness with a leaning towards world-weariness. As a significant stratagem, a witch will probe for tell-tale marks fencing the ridge of footloose Hermes. This part of the palm shows a love of change, travel, as well as a rapidity of thought, even though a fullness of the mound warns of evil inclinations. Perhaps that is why most witches move swiftly to the crescent of Selene. A strongly dappled pad demonstrates an idealistic or romantic personality. Conversely, cratered carvings show sensitivity, coupled with a love of nocturnal sophistication. The last portion of the palm to be read is the rise of Aphrodite, because it relates to uncontrolled lust, or warmth of temperament. Unique etchings are then finally taken into account, such as birthmarks, the texture of the skin, and the overall shape of the arm. At this point, witches remind their clients that the left hand (on a right handed person), is chiselled with previous behaviour patterns. A right hand however, changes with the course of present experience.

Caliban's dam Sycorax taught him physiognomy and phrenology, because a client's facial features and cranial shape may be analogically compared to those of an animal. As Wiccan diagnoses, readings are based on an ageless perception that human beings recapitulate the entire evolutionary process, despite the fact that the vast majority of people only progress to rudimentary stages. Demonstrably, everyone reflects the juncture at which an adaptation-chain stopped, and this proves to be the esoteric key unlocking their essential qualities. Hence, an "ape-headed" man is mischievous and fun loving, but lacks determination and stability. A "lion-headed" adolescent is a person of natural courage, though one who acts in a foolhardy fashion. His dam's private journal further mentioned, "ass-headed" women who are stubborn, stupid and loyal, along with "pig-headed" babies who are ruled by their base appetites. They also detailed an unevenness on the right side of a "donkey-shaped skull", indicated congenital pride, "bequeathed" by overly assertive ancestors. A Craft remedy for this, she had written, would be to empathise with other people, thereby stimulating the alternative side of the cranium.

With these skills in mind, Caliban looked closely at the stooping couple in front of him. Increasingly shocked, his earthly eyes awoke to the realisation that Helen (the groom), was a living weapon against the tyranny of rationalism, quite unlike her step-sister Moscow Chestnova of recent Soviet history. His Helen stood at the candle-lit altar like a legendary Scottish Hag:

her extended chin, arching forehead and huge crook nose embodying rebellion. For her special day, Helen wore an extremely tight, green, ball gown, exaggerating her hunched back and causing her to mutter in barely suppressed curses. Against their better judgement, the congregation watched Helen's androgynous frame tremble, as though she were a suspended marionette with hands quivering upwards in a series of disturbing mudras. Guests seated nearby were further unnerved at Helen's tiny teeth, as wan as parsnips, and on permanent, malicious, display. Like a modern day Mother Shipton among the elect, Helen revelled in grotesquery.

Confusingly, her partner Emily (the bride), was a much more powerful witch. In appearance she was tall, lean and boyish, partly explaining why her dress sense never stretched beyond tweeds. However, Emily's heavily bespectacled face always retained its expression of Sapphic superiority. Indeed, to the congregation, her every move appeared strangely slow and precise, like a collection of sepia photographs. Emily's intimates, including Caliban, commented that she had an atmosphere about her, similar to the menace posed by an angry colony of Africanised Bees. The threat she personified seemed inconsequential until it was aroused to devastating effect, and since most people at the Service were Emily's friends, or family, it came as no surprise that the girls audibly cackled at each other as they exchanged their vows.

Suddenly, the dwarf felt his huge imaginal hands beginning to move of their own accord: they now had strength enough to strike down all his clerical oppressors. In a moment, Caliban understood the sleepless nights of the Christian Ascetics, the physical privations of Indian Fakirs and the icy baths taken by young Tibetan Monks as methods to reinforce this imaginal superstructure. If he wished to use his imaginal fists to punch his opponent's imaginal stomachs, he could knock them across the room with no discernable cause. Likewise, Caliban speculated that if he intended to kill the clerics, he could fashion a shard of black light into imaginal daggers and ecstatically plunge them into his inquisitor's imaginal backs. No orthodox physician could detect the cause of his enemie's deterioration, still less have the requisite knowledge, or necessary power, to remove these subtle weapons. Only another witch of equal ability would be able to perform the task without adding more problems to the case. Perhaps the Instituto di Psicosintesi alone knew how to heal such wounds.

Immediately afterwards, Caliban's imaginal eyes opened wide. He saw the Saint of Saints, Christed Esus, and realised all three of The Healers bodies were woven together in the archetypal world. Caliban sensed Esus' movements in the iconography behind the clerics. He saw a man at Gethsemane whom he will never forget. He observed his unkempt hair, crippled carriage and Semitic nose. Caliban marvelled at the Saint's gigantic heart-shaped head, single Cyclopean eye, and muscled, luminous torso. He detected the white rainment of a skilled Therapeutae and he thought he heard oral prescriptions. Caliban saw him picking a cluster of nearly unrecognisable weeds, as well as Hemp and black pods. The dwarf felt an immense need to reach out and touch The Healer, but refused to embarrass himself. Caliban could taste in his mouth a supper of Goose and Claret held in Esus' honour, and became festive at the flavour. He realised this celestial Saint was the Lord of Infinite Space, who could hide himself in a cobnut shell. Miraculously, The Healer had transcended material limitation.

Caliban started to understand imaginal space as the source of Witchcraft, because the Gnostic Name of our Goddess echoes everywhere in those dimensions. Her sighs constitute a Symphonic Grimoire, recorded by witches in the organic world as transcripts forming a Book of Reverberation. Although young witches are often heard to moan with frustrated reverence that these sounds are frequently misheard, which is why the study of their notational grammar gave potentially life-threatening knowledge. For Caliban in particular, the error of Classical Civilisation was to put so-called musical expertise on a pedestal and subsequently project its fallible pronouncements as if they were descriptions of a fixed reality. Older witches constantly added to the debate that everything in the earthly realm was relatively true and that Vibration is actually the agent securing each sigil, or trapping human cognition. Grammar and foreground static aren't the same thing.

The effects of his drug were wearing off and Caliban didn't know whether a hundred seconds or a hundred years had passed. Noises loudly played their music in his ears, making him feel slightly sickly. Nonetheless, he quickly recovered himself in order to greet his friend. "Congratulations Emily, how does it feel to be an unlawfully married woman?"

"Utterly great!"

"Where is your other half?"

"She's trying to avoid Uncle Newty and the artful bodger."

"Ah!" Caliban guessed that the latter was Helen's brother AKA "the loser." He also felt he was expected to say something portentous, such as "people don't always recognise when they fall in love, and are normally incapable of doing the right thing once they have." But this was a time to celebrate and he needed to make his way to the garden with the other guests. As he did he chanted about this Iconic Experience beneath his breath:

"Miltonic superb-ungradable; utterly, completely. Miltonic perfect-ungradable; totally, absolutely. Miltonic clever-gradable; very, rather, exceptionally. Miltonic interesting-gradable; rather, most, very."

I grew up with your shocking foreign tongue

I grew up with you and yes, ignored you.

As it flicked its threatening fork

In corner newsagents and language academies,

While drowning stars regressed inward,

Evermore downward, and evermore deeply,

Through a multi-culture of murky veils

Wrapping marzipan boys in Wahhabi nostalgia

As they struggle with our silvered service

Across infidel knave and pert pink nipple

Both Kafir and evermore heathen

Yet still licking sour Britons to the liberal rear

With exact rimming for paranoid bodies

To then brag their treason in sordid Soukous

Amongst damaged nightmares and endarkening tracts.

His Green Italian Owl

Entering the overgrown two-acre garden felt like stepping into a haunted forest. The difference being that Caliban was instantly greeted by a drop-dead gorgeous waiter, holding a silver tray with brimming pink-champagne glasses. He must have been about twenty-four years old, with devastatingly handsome Italian looks, an athletic build and an extremely personable manner. His ponytail crowned a natural nobility, which was further diademed by expensive Gucci sunglasses. Caliban knew the boy wanted to talk, and only held himself back because of the black grease paint all over his face: a theatrical touch that strangely threw his pursed, sensuous lips into an exaggerated, although sculpted, relief. It also seemed to magnify his piercing brown eyes, as oracular as any Owls, making manifest barely repressed bi-sexual sentiments. Aroused, the dwarf decided to break any uneasy conversational ice: "What's your name young man?"

"Karmine, Karmine Klossowski," he smiled.

"That doesn't sound very Mediterranean," Caliban smiled back.

"It is useful as a waiter to sound-ah eastern European since political Enlargement."

"Very smart, does it work?"

"Yes usually, forgive me…they-ah say…you are a witch!"

"People say all sorts of things, however in this case they are indirectly correct. Actually, I am a physical medium, but why do you ask?" Again Karmine smiled, only this time his mouth betrayed a mixture of lust and longing.

"They-ah say…when you have had a witch, no one else-ah will do."

"Sometimes what they say is right," Caliban replied, cautiously.

"Lets-ah walk together and talk about-ah the trees. Witches know-ah a lot about the trees and the verdant coppice and-ah the fertility."

"And you must tell me why the girls wanted their waiting staff dressed like a troupe of Mummers. Follow me to the Holly hedges over there." Caliban could hardly believe what was happening, and as they strolled together began to prove his Craft credentials to the young libertine.

"There are thirteen living consonants and five vital vowels to the Old Goidelic tree alphabet. The first organic letter of the series is the tree of inception, so-called because Birch is the earliest tree (with the macabre exception of the sinister Alder), to sprout new leaves each year. It was said that to beat someone with birch twigs would expel the infirm spirits who continually delight in causing insanity and mayhem: a method intimately connected with the practice of marking village boundaries with birch-rods. Increased clarity is therefore the key to its arcane properties, as well as the power of protection." Caliban pointed to a withered, palled, Birch. They both took a sip of Champagne.

Still walking, Caliban then pointed to the other uncultivated side of the path, while admiring Karmine's agility as he placed his tray gracefully down without any glasses falling over. The boy moved with a sinuous skill, like a sophisticated urban Stoat on heat. "Wicked Willow is the fifth tree to be catalogued by the occult sages of old, and accordingly Culpeper says the Moon owns it. By this he seems to suggest that the Willow always enjoyed a dread reputation, representing the forces of misery and bleak misfortune. Antiquarians further claim human sacrifices were offered to unclean spirits in baskets made of Willow, while for centuries wearing a Willow hat signalled the intense hatred of a rejected lover. Even today, the poorest families still hesitate to use it for domestic firewood. Its sap however is its secret, since this disturbing liquid can be used to spread communal discord and physical decay." Karmine dreamily nodded towards the heavily shaded end of the path and started to unbutton his red cotton shirt. "But it's the seventh tree," Caliban unflappably continued, "the alphabets Royal Heart, whose anthropomorphic qualities constantly unsettle the simple-minded. This is due to the fact Oak shrieks and groans when felled. Midsummer kindling is nevertheless always Oaken, because its intoxicating smoke awakens physical strength as well as spiritual determination. Oak, I should continue, has a wide range of potencies: its sap may be used to preserve youth or rejuvenate sexual vigour, and if an Oak branch is made into a Will-Projecting Wand, it protects a witch from lightening, detection and exhaustion. Moreover, a bronze nail driven into the correct engrams inscribed on its regal trunk relieve a person of any physical pain; immediately curing minor ailments such as toothache. Oddly, even Farmers remain unaware that eyesight is extended when its powdered bark is brewed with soft poppy seeds and stale, necrotic, saliva, into a nocturnally administered tincture." They were a long way down the garden by now and far from the other guests. Caliban physically felt Karmine's hot, bare stomach against his shoulders, and pausing briefly, they both savoured the seductive moment.

"As the ninth tree," Caliban said breathily while taking his own purple shirt off, "Hazel is held to be wisdom's emblam, since forked Hazel spears (which must be cut on St. John's Eve), are used to look for lost treasure or employed to identify thieves and murderers. Additionally, Hazel twigs are wielded by diviners when they are looking for hidden sources of water, metals buried beneath the ground, or dead bodies. There are even recipes for making oneself invisible by applying a magnetised herbal ointment over the body and carrying a Mandrake talisman with green Hazel twigs inserted into it, at the Angle-Of-Deception. Folklorists occasionally recounted the phenomenon wherein decaying Hazel twigs sometimes drip poisonous milk exuding paralysing vapours capable of killing untold thousands. It is said that witches alone can safely approach the Hazel during this period". Karmine physically pulled Caliban into a secluded nook behind the Holly hedges, while rapidly stripping himself naked. He wiped away the grease paint with his vest and untied the rainbow ribbons damming a flood of long black hair.

"I am-ah a political activist for-ah the Greens. We need-ah to remember the land and-ah its ways". Forcibly, he undressed Caliban. "We need-ah to honour muscle and-ah the blood in ourselves; to respect-ah the oxygen producing plants-ah and-ah the soil. To recover the-ah economics of Eden is not-ah the function of an impotent-ah body of representatives. All that can-ah be hoped-ah for, from such an-ah artificial organism, is that it-ah will represent the totality of-ah visceral reaction's proclaimed-ah by the people. The bad-ah airs we now-ah breath stink in our own lungs as-ah though we wanted to asphyxiate ourselves-ah with our own filth." Karmine surveyed him sharply, waiting for a reaction. Under such scrutiny, Caliban felt like a salted slug oozing its inadequacy in the dust before this magnificent man: an ugly creature encouraging loathing and disgust in the presence of a resplendent satyr. They were both further excited by this shared, abusive, impression.

Uncharacteristically, the dwarf stammered in response, "the tenth, tenth…shit… esoteric tree is the Vine in its vintage season. It embodies joy, exhilaration and righteous wrath. Any, any, any student of Craft is alerted to the sorcerous properties of the Vine, because of its traditional link with the devil. This, coupled with the f-f-fact that there is a lusty symbolism … oh! …surrounding the Vine, offers valuable clues to its particular gifts: the primitive plea-sure of drunken violence as a means to achieve magical states of consciousness. For this reason Paracelsus writes that rituals worked with sour wine are unusually effective in raising power. Indeed, applied ceremonial contention may…shit…be used…shit, boy.. to channel subtle energies in a highly concentrated way, as the well-trained practitioners of any martial art will readily testify." Adrenaline energised Caliban's blood stream. They found themselves naked, embracing, kissing.

Being literally brushed off his feet as they tried to pin each other down on the grass, Caliban pulled Karmine's hair and mumbled, "Ivy in its flowering season is the eleventh esoteric tree. In ancient Rome, Ivy was chewed by soldiers seeking homicidal

High Brooms

Of a sudden, a Sylph woke Caliban from his bubbly bed. From behind his right ear he heard the loud creaking of an Chestnut door, which cursed the fact it was still closed by moaning and barking in splintered tones,

"Struggled sanctuary; compared to animal teeth, actively hurting the hierophant." Caliban thought Chestnut monads assumed far too much, but was interested enough to start searching for this braggart. From the corner of his now captivated left eye, he noticed two horizontal cellar doors in the ground near the North wall of the church. How could he not have noticed them before? They looked both heavy and huge, with wrought iron seals to bar entry to the uninvited. Nonetheless, Caliban sensed part of the reason he had been asked as a guest to this wedding was beneath those beckoning beams.

He ceremoniously walked to the cellar, knelt over the padlocks and struck the imprisoning metal chains with his Athame, forcing them to release their grip on the monad. Immediately, Caliban felt relief emanating from the wood. When he had cautiously opened the grateful doors, Caliban then descended a Chestnut staircase into an enormous storehouse of books and artefacts. He saw a cabinet prepared for materialisations, tin trumpets for spirit voices and all the paraphernalia of late Victorian séance rooms, including obligatory Aspidistras, Broomsticks, Planchettes and Antimacassars placed neatly on well-upholstered seats. Without warning, Caliban felt an invisible swirl of monads forming and reforming; attempting to construct as well as reshape themselves into former configurations. They emitted a noise in their commotion, sounding strangely like the Divine Word "Aum".

One of the trumpets immediately floated to his left ear, allowing the ghostly presence of Sir John Leicester to wail, "all arguments are provisional, and Britain doesn't exist." Caliban held his breath as the voice continued, "Perhaps that is why there has never really been a scientific theory which has stood the test of time. It may also partly explain the often bewildering personal ambiguities surrounding those figures representing each school of Perennial Thought. In modern Spiritism, for example, the Fox sisters are usually cited as the ancestors of our tradition, even though some commentators vigorously claim it was actually Emanuel Swedenborg who fathered the movement. Yet a cursory glance at the beliefs as well as the practices of Spiritism – as a coherent ideology – quickly reveals a religious system of global proportions as old as the human race itself. Therefore, it is a striking, albeit unsettling fact, that temporary frames of reference tend to dominate our rules of judgement." Unexpectedly, the trumpet fell to the ground.

Caliban had read this is equally true of those opinions said to oppose Spiritisms theological position. Indeed, until recently existentialism was held up by a series of secularised scholars as a bulwark against any notion entailing higher states of Being. By stating they were following the – surprisingly reductive – assertions of Neitzsche, these writers created an impression that theirs was the only possible way to discuss human spirituality – thereby deliberately ignoring the equally important religious existentialism of Kierkegaard. Caliban pondered, as a member of the Balder Fellowship, that it constantly depressed him to reflect that they had not fully engaged with the sophisticated and rich theological resources generally available. Clearly, as a Spiritist family they had a surprising number of prominent friends, and it is far from uncommon to find authors such as Saint Augustine and Pascal listed as existential thinkers who described profound transcendent experiences.

"Existentialism is then," called out a semi-manifest Doctor Cheong, "best understood as a certain type of poetic exploration, tending to focus on the human situation itself. Moreover, most writers inspired by this vantage point have gone on to contend that western thinking has become deeply defective due to its increasing insistence that knowledge must be based on physical objects alone. For a true existentialist, this approach will never be able to grasp the unique spiritual nature of human beings and remains blinded to the immense differences between human and non-human Being. A view which gave birth to a twentieth century academic rebellion in Italy (curiously known as Christian Existentialism), that sought to examine people as much more than mere bags of chemicals." The spirit-person disappeared without any warning in a cloud of ectoplasm.

"Presumably, channelling is a case in point," interjected Caliban's living guide the Tibetan, D.K from the rafters.

"Everyone seems to channel. Suddenly thinking of an old friend before "accidentally" meeting her on a street corner, or spontaneously singing a memorable song only to hear it played on the radio moments later, are all examples of this very human aptitude. Yet the difference between these suggestive daily events and those exhibiting spiritual qualities is ultimately one of degree. For a busy English housewife this ability may be a question of mild intuitive feedback, whereas for a Sufi Poet this disturbing process allows prophetic spirits to expose unpalatable truths. On top of this, inherited customs with no direct moral significance such as New Years Eve, allow entire societies to channel glimpses of their own future and foretell the probable consequences of actions still to be undertaken. Such predictions are of course, both subjective and falsifiable, consequently raising higher metaphysical issues in their wake. Perhaps this is one of the reasons why some channellers have opened themselves enough to touch the glittering continuum itself, subsequently writing that they discovered a changing, dynamic and ever-living universe with an inherent forward thrust towards the full actualisation of every potential from which it is composed. They almost seem to be describing dazzling creative acts in terms of a continuous birth process by powers and principalities above all human interference. And I should add there are no British Isles." There was a long silence whereupon Caliban speculated why the spirits repeatedly said his country didn't exist.

Without warning, the fricative tones of Silver Birch rang out to say, "Now it is always wise to be cautious concerning the euphoric details accompanying these descriptions. After all, outward expressions of such purely receptive insights are bound to use special figurative and symbolic terms, which no doubt imply far more than appears to be said at first hearing, but are still, nevertheless, semantically problematic. This is due to the fact that ordinary words are made for mundane occasions and cannot convey the extraordinary facts of Spiritism. What is more, these symbols refer to levels of consciousness that are more complex than the everyday empirical world, going far beyond the physical limits of recognisable, material, conditions - which is why the city of London doesn't exist." Caliban had heard that intelligence expands in the hereafter, and marvelled at this morbid, although perplexing commentary.

The whirlwind of monads became stronger. "My taken name is Zodiac," said a louder, more plosive, voice. "In stretching so high, yet simultaneously embracing the dislocation of human beings here below, our movement (considered as an entirety), is unique. This is because Spiritist churches meet existential questions head-on. They are sacred arenas of raw human need, where the bereaved, the marginalized, the misfortunate and the uneducated can congregate, freely express themselves and openly enquire into the meaning of their lives without fear of censure or social disapproval. Unlike more culturally established religious assemblies, where every member has a perceived – and tacitly understood – place in the social pecking order, spiritists are drawn together by their pain and curiosity. We have an innate religious bond built on unadulterated spiritual experiences and honest vulnerability. Without warning, a Ouija Board was thrown from a table nearby. It smashed against a bookcase, and rolled to the corner of the room.

"At the end of the day my dear Caliban", whispered the beloved voice of Red Feather, "spiritism claims there is a higher order of Being, and by so arguing states that our lives may be understood in two distinct ways: either as a scientific problem requiring a solution, or as a mystery within which we choose to participate. In other words, human rules of judgement are based on a materialistic, apparently clear but radically impoverished views of existence ... or on a transcendent, less explicable – although fundamentally meaningful – interaction with all of creation. Surely there is no better way to state our theological position than this, and equally no more courageous way to face the future." With this, the maelstrom of monads began to ease, and then fall into the sweetest of silences.

Caliban raised his arms in a gesture of gratitude and bowed to this august assembly. Yet a feeling of anxiety had entered his heart. Anxiety, as well as an almost traumatised trembling. The spirits had offered a deeply disturbing augur, making him speculate that he may ever see his home again. Perhaps that was why, when Caliban turned and ascended the chestnut stairs, back into the twilight of a late evening wedding reception, he found himself muttering about the survival of the brightest. He also wondered if anyone had noticed his prolonged, mysterious, absence?

Dark the dawn, but bright the day,

I drained the bitter dregs full draught

Of sweetly honeysuckled indecisions,

Coming home to heart and hearth.

While praising Old English Spirits

With Mead, with serenades,

And with kisses.

And like the ever-mysterious Bee in bliss

Whose world is dewdrop and blossom

Began a War Dance, ever wielded

Like a weapon to wound and whittle

Away my wolfish antagonists;

And embodying the strength

To defend my Motherland; to deliver my

Own Kith and Kindred.

Through muscular moves as perfectible

As heraldic analogy, when orchestrating

New Burgundian victories

Above both Rust and Gravity.

Questioning Tate Britain

"All aboard for London."

Caliban could hardly believe he was finally hearing those words as he approached the marquis for a second time. The girls had obviously left hours earlier, shortly after cutting the cake. Everyone, apart from him, had given their sincerest blessing and wished them both a very happy honeymoon. They, in turn, had promised punctual transport back to the various cities that their guests had come from. With that promise in mind, Caliban joyfully heard the clarion call again: "All aboard. Can you start making your way to the coach for London now, please." The driver was very slight and strangely gaunt, with a long, bony, finger, pointing at the vehicle - although Caliban hardly noticed him. From the dwarf's perspective, this wedding felt more like an odyssey than a celebration. When he had first arrived in Liverpool his hang-over made his thunderous mood irrasible, but that was before arguing with his spirit guides, an Italian seduction and the copious amounts of Champagne.

"All aboard." The bilious driver himself entered the coach, checked passenger numbers, and then took his seat to begin their journey. Caliban observed that outside the vehicle a thick fog was forming, which, inexplicably, made him feel uneasy. He also saw his colleague G.I. Joe sat near the eminent Sexologist Angelo Junior. Unsurprisingly, Caliban's Armenian friend looked the worse for ware on Putinka and was already eating raw onions, while mumbling about Fontainbleau. Caliban did his best to quietly ignore him, along with Will Sinclair and J.B Gallard resting at the back near David Icke.

"Och now, don't ye think that in his manuscript Transcendental Magic," interjected Philemon, a wise-old-winged-man with bull's horns, and holding four keys seated behind him, "The occultist Eliphas Levi reiterates an unfair, although quite historical distinction between someone who lives as a Magician and another who lives as a witch? Eh? Aye, okay, the overly conservative Levi thought a Magician works with a force revealed by Divine Science for the good of humanity, whereas witches give themselves to impure spirits, since they practise an infernal art seeking to manipulate both nature and the human brain for personal gain." Caliban politely listened, but was angry.

"Aye, this curious division of disciplines goes all the way back to the Holy Bible itself," continued Philemon, "where, in the acts of the Apostles, if ye don't mind me saying, the pious read of a confrontation between the witch Elymas and the Preacher Paul. It is there written that Elymas is accused of deceit, legerdemain and the abuse of his power by a man who proceeds to curse him by temporarily taking away his sense of sight. This, of course, simply reflects a difference in discipline to the so-called forbidden knowledge. One arbitrarily moralising on its application, due to the fact that a practitioner embraces the ethical system of a particular culture, while the other approach uses an experimental and analytic method, striving to rise above the limitations of every possible society." Outside the coach, numbing fog further obscured the road, buildings, and even suburban lawns.

"Aye, aye, this is one of the reasons why a witch like yerself spends so much time meditating upon the dynamics of the human soul as a veritable speculum for all future understanding. Ye'll moreover realise there are a large number of personalities at work within the psyche of every living person, some of which are more helpful to a witch than others. Concomitantly, all of these different aspects of the human spirit form an inner hierarchy that is vital to the unfolding of our individual monad, an elative substance that could be called the 'cunning-self'. Aye, the very depths of its being are composed of tricksters, jesters and method actors on the stage of manifestation. Ergo, witches have customarily been referred to as 'clever' or 'manipulative'. Philemon raised his first key towards an increasingly obscure celestial canopy.

"This is certainly revealed in the life-style choices of a modern witch, who adjusts to each new set of circumstances as they arise, in the knowledge that these 'truths' are transitory and will pass with the centuries. Hats-off-to-ye, witches say only love and freedom are worth struggling for in this or any other life. It is no accident thereby, that the techniques of Mediumship often resemble patterns of behaviour expressed by people in their early childhood. Och, I didnay mention play fighting and sand castles in my preamble! Clearly though, children tend to have a structural familiarity with the connective principles behind mediumistic expression, whilst lacking the sheer determination of an adult to make these facilities work. In this sense, mediums seek to regain the unsophisticated creativity, adaptability and deeply imagistic transference, necessary to achieve real power. Aye, oh, aye, from this perspective it suddenly becomes increasingly obvious that Mediumship depends on exploiting the psychic links between different aspects of consciousness." Caliban felt magically assaulted, but began to realise how little he knew about the relation between his psyche and the greater physical world around him. His felt-senses told him that outside the coach everything was melting away into indistinct shapes, colours, a toxic smell and finally the taste of putrescence. Philemon held up a second key.

Bucking up courage, Caliban asked, "What is Britain?"

"What are you, boy?"

An uneasy silence passed between them.

"Do you understand my comment?"

"I canne be sure."

"What do you mean, not sure?"

"This ... not sure mind ... is the subconscious. For a nominally Christian spirit such as I, any question about geography is really about the self." Philemon fingered a third key.

"Is that all Britain is then?" exclaimed Caliban., "A confusion of ethnic identities? Are you claiming that's what I am?"

"Isn't that enough to begin with? Spiritism is not about dead people, but the Eternal Self; discovered in endless locations and scenarios. That is why this Holy territory, and perhaps particularly England's own Pre-Anglo-Saxon capital city of Londinium, doesn't exist in itself. To this very day, some see it as a city of commerce. For others, it is a university city. Foreigner visitors travel there due to a belief that London is the centre of the dramatic world, whereas natives know it's clubs and pubs embody the international capital of Rock Music. Soon, London will be the city of Polish day dreams; tomorrow it will be Londonobad."

Another, more difficult silence passed between them.

"Okay, one plus one equals two," Caliban grumbled.

"That's good. Aye. The Truth is very simple, Aye, but any comprehension of that truth is extremely complex."

"Meaning?"

"Sex and spirit define the depths of self, not architecture and duration. Och, each life on this external plane is only a clarification of both, despite repressed Victorian traders doing their absolute damndest to dilute these twinned, hallowed, experiences." Philemon sat back in his seat, seemingly exhausted by the exchange. He looked a little less distinct than he had when this unelicited conversation had begun. Caliban, on the other hand, realised that the spirit-person had pinpointed his problem. If he didn't embrace his ethnicity, he would never evolve beyond it. At that very moment, the coach seemed to stop shaking and glide along invisible roads that curled in on themselves. Space collapsed. The motorway melted, while the London orbital crumbled into the remnants of a chidding stone. Caliban didn't know whether his fellow passengers could see these signs or not, but got up and begged the driver to stop outside Tate Britain, since the final Ring-Pass-Not to his mystical journey lay within that building.

Dark Mother Nothing once

Cradled her Shadow babies

Who talked about Olympic defeats

And terrorist yesterdays.

A few even awarded themselves

Shadow cash for shadow honours

In penumbral apartments atop

The overshadowed electorate.

But in their shaded silences

When shadow hopes, as shadow fears,

Seem more solid and certain, they

Raged against the Saxon Dawn

Wherein a Golden Light will one day

Morning.

Thus, each now blindly broods

During their shadowy evenings

About Oriental Poisons

In a suddenly hostile and depressing city.

Lord Heimdall's Revealing

Caliban leapt from the coach, ran up the semi-solid stone stairs and tumbled through the rapidly revolving glass doors to the gallery, finding himself declaiming:

"Avert your eyes."

Caliban then seized a grey ceremonial gown draped over a nearby bust of Turner in the portico. There was a huge red cross of St. George embroidered on its hood as well as a loaded .380 ACP pistol in its pocket. Again, he stormed;

"Avert your eyes, do, really, absolutely, completely."

Caliban jumped in the air and deliberately fell to the floor in a martial dance of defiance, knowing that he had to begin his duel at once for the banishing ritual to expel the stale atmosphere of corrupt centuries. Yet Caliban unexpectedly heard the cocophony of faceless celebrities at a noisy exhibition in the main hall. The only sculptor present, Grayson Perry, may have remarked;

"There are no Lance Corporals in the Guards, dear boy. It goes back to Victoria's time, when she wouldn't have … ch ??? ….. the…,"

'But … abo!!!!! … the Basingstoke cannel. …" mouthed back Claire and Eadweard Muybridge, apparently almost in unison.

Undeterred however, by these disconcerting snippets of civilised conversation (similar to flies around the magnificently antlered, although already rotting carcass of Western Arts), Caliban's Thaumatergical Will remained implacable. He rolled across the floor before jumping to his feet again and wailing;

"Avert your eyes with what and all."

The deafened celebrities seemed to assume he was a performance artist and carried on drinking wine, which suited Caliban as he purposefully started the process of expulsion by afterwards decrying;

"There is a transcendent principle. It is encountered within every work of art, most music, literature, and all the Great Religions. On occasion, it even surfaces in the sciences when visionary theories pierce the structure of creation, allowing our human intellects to delve more deeply into the world's material processes. This spiritual consciousness, however, primarily takes ecological shapes and environmental forms: it sings in the symphonies of the Dawn Chorus; it enlightens its own splendour in the glories of a golden sunset. If therefore, as some saints have said, these are the lavish signs of a Divine Soul crucified on the cross of materiality, then we must assume that such an immense sacrifice is leading to a shared, cosmic, perfection. Only this would explain the endless moments of uplifting regeneration in a belittlingly beautiful universe." By this time, the dissolving corridors had become translucent, taking on the appearance of endless crystalline caverns stretching backwards into infinity. Caliban further noticed that in these strangely sheltered spaces, modern hunter gathering men were finding for their mates the occasional article to read, and digest, while the paintings surrounding them were like the first, or maybe the very last, abstract thoughts of our aesthetically uneasy species.

At that thought, Caliban mewled even more loudly,

"This also partly explains why indigenous British customs often appear analogous to a spiritual habitat rather than a mere political mechanism. In a sense, they comprise a synthetic genius, raising us to previously unexpected heights. Certainly, our inherited and temperate values can neither be cropped, or culled, nor can they be cleared away like unwanted bracken. After all, British folk-feelings have emerged from lush native soils, laboured over by our stubborn ancestors, who cultivated these lands for centuries untold; ancestors who themselves pollinated fertile traditions with good humour, while husbanding our inherited, verdant, resources. It was the poets among them however, who defiantly channelled the disembodied moods of this 'folk-spirit' into the verbal icons and passionate chants illuminating national sentiment." Caliban noted that each gallery wall reflected (like a brilliant facet inside an enormous diamond), the image of endless, as well as nameless, celebrities; but Caliban still couldn't locate his opponent's position. Desperately, the dwarf redoubled his efforts, while pushing away the sickening image that some of the celebrities were silencing their discount desires by chewing dried flesh between ice teeth.

As a repulsive battle cry, Caliban wailed;

"The social necessity of this Sacred Service was of course, always a matter of turbulent political dispute. Among early Anglo-Saxon settlers for example, controversy surrounded the fact that there were few sacrosanct Master Poets, but a plenitude of roving minstrels – despite the enduring inspiration of the Eddas and Old Norse scholarship. As they acclimatised, English poetic lore became heavily embellished at third hand by Welsh, Irish and Gallic Olaves through the Norman Romances – cultural events helping to contextualise the fact that there has never been an intuitive respect for the title of poet in England. Adding further confusion to injury, English poets as a body (since that time), have tended to feel apologetic regarding their vocation, and more often than not have described their calling as 'writer' or 'teacher' instead of wordsmith. Despite this, great poets did arise out of humble English stock: Coleridge; George, The Lord Byron and Keats, being second to none in world literature; quite possibly because the Mediumistic origins of pure English poetry were never entirely forgotten.

"But, with so few Master Poets the demands of our tribal psyche became increasingly opaque, even though a collective sense of its activities continued to haunt society. Imperatives and taboos! Hence, hardly anyone, including the 'official' clergy, spoke authoratatively on these elevated matters, or attempted to guide general debate; a silence which almost deafened English cultural life. Moreover, on those occasions when the Transcendent Principle did blaze through our affairs, these Epiphanic Moments seemed akin to pagan outbursts instead of perennial signs within a tradition already exhibiting an uncanny continuity. Somewhat predictably, religious puritans found themselves increasingly wary of the English festal calendar, causing a paralysing spiritual dichotomy in our seasonal customs. These seizures however, proved to be a period of poetic opportunity during which Poet-Mediums spent their lives trying to use this schism to restore the Great-Theme-of-Intentional-Suffering as the story of our Western World. Personally, they lived Romantic lives of excess and debauched immolation. Equally, they wrote of Royal Anfortas, the Fisher-King, and even upheld ethnic Britains as the Ever-Wounded-Servants of all Nations."

Caliban circled and circled and circled, scrying on the glittering fragments of ceiling above him, before throwing himself through the mezzanine doors to the left. He reached for his pistol and tornadoed once again; "Avert your eyes, whatever, what on Earth!"

Caliban then jumped down the staircase in three enormous summersaults until he was in the marble basement. Caliban ignored the fatuous celebrities milling to and fro and up and down, although he cautiously made the sign of Miollnir to protect himself. Behind the cloakroom Caliban saw dark, guilty, cocaine-drenched images behaving suspiciously. Against them he hexed; "Whatever the underlying social causes, to pretend as contemporary liberals tend to, that ethnicity doesn't exist, or that it is irrelevant, is simply vexing as well as counter intuitive in an endarkening way. It is, after all, rare to meet a Chinese businessman or an Israeli scholar who is not proud to inherit their cultural identity, let alone acknowledge physical descent from their familial line; not to mention Jamaican Boxers or Pakistani accountants. Also, my Polish friends have reminded me, in all seriousness, that other ethnic groups seem more important to the British than our own 'material kind'; a question that is far from facile – and on closer inspection demands grave reflection. Neither present day guilt, nor previous trade links, fully explain the disproportionate social representation afforded certain minorities in this country, and disguise a disturbing global agenda. A conspiracy started in Victorian London and exemplified by you, Sir John Tate." Caliban pointed an accusatory finger at the talismanic skull being venerated by overdressed, ageing, celebrities, who reeled at this cyclonic accusation. Caliban quickly held his pistol with both hands and shot the barbarous bone, as through performing the ancient procedure of trepanation. Instantly, there was a flash of rainbow light, or Heimdall's-Revealed-Holiness as his Clan would once have whispered, followed by a renewed sense of solidity and substance trickling from Tate's otherwise poisonous marrow. Caliban knew that Right-Perspective had been released and was restoring order in the world around him.

He put his pistol away and tried to comfort the mindless, shocked, celebrities, who were moving as randomly as abandoned puppets by explaining;

"Ethnicity is neither an accident nor an inconvenience; it is one of the foundations of our British Being, both ethnicity and words. Moreover, attempts to grasp our British Bulldog by his ears and rise above ethnicity demands that these fleshly facts be fully embraced as the Touchstone-Of-The-Ages … no matter how many millennia this magical process of transformation takes. Otherwise a strangely pestilent and prohibited diminution seizes hold of those who mistakenly claim they have left its limitations behind. We are ethnically, what we are in potential. Perhaps that is one of the reasons why the greatest Anglo-Saxon Witch is the English language herself. She has, after all, matured in evolving mouths through the centuries from Her origins as a brutish warrior's spittle, into a truly articulate and sophisticated Mother Tongue. In this capacity, She has stirred Her lexical cauldrons on every continent in a Grimoire of transmuted texts; which is far from surprising when considering English ceased to belong to one Island or population long ago. In this sense, it is only Her children's exceptional capacity for abstract thought that enables students of language to conceive of English as a single incantation. This is equally true of American, Canadian and Australian who have become mature, independent, daughters. Indeed, our Mother Tongue has even given birth to colourful Pidgins and bright coal black Creoles, often nursed in less than favoured wordscapes. Wherever Her presence, She still gifts the blessing of Anglo-Saxon consciousness to those who seek genuine Spiritual progress." As he said this, Caliban moved to the side entrance and opened the chromium doors, already sensing the luminous dawn of a reconstructing day.

They've gone from my whitened face

To a better place I know

Beyond every icon of evil,

But gone, far far, away

From my peripheral vision

And from behind my heavy head.

To somewhere utterly Subjective

Without a gradable touch or tactile pleasure

Or moments wreathed by Chlorophyll tears.

Since Eternity had neither been postponed

Nor cancelled until a propitious Tuesday

The rain sodden week after next

Where there are no Forget-Me-Nots

Or masks of rainbow wire

Disguising their tragically predestined pain.

A Postscript Of Valentines

From the pen of St. Caliban, both grace and mercy: Rainbow Radiance has entered my head, revealing The Goddess within me. Cum luce salutem! I have seen Our Lady PSYCHE, and found She wears innumerable masks. She is Many and She is One. Perhaps this is the very reason why I no longer believe that these strikingly different manifestations are of little or no consequence to Englishmen, since to us she is Ostara, or the subjective side of matter. Each Easter we remember Her Miracle as New Life comes out of death, and certainly without this sense of Immanent Orientation, only the deepest of cultural confusions can result. Therefore, let me nail my ideological colours to the Cathedral door from the beginning. I have travelled through the woods from being a mere Pagan proselyte to become a Heathen Priest. In this vocational capacity, I recognise aspects of Our Goddess everywhere, but perhaps particularly in my own people, and when I notice in them another poet, he or she becomes my own true Valentine.

These Valentine verses are, consequently, written with the deepest reverence as literary keep-sakes to my Brothers and Sisters in Gnosis, or in other words, as a nod to their potent spiritual influences on my work. Certainly, from the beginning of my journey, our Heathen Religious Imagination reminded me that every flowering bud is a dew drenched totem of desire and attraction; which is precisely why, along with the sages of old, I embrace everything that is sexually beautiful. Albeit on the understanding that complex literary, religious and moral issues cannot, or should not, be avoided in societies name. Or put more succinctly, devalued by a literary establishment increasingly draconian as well as intolerant towards any opinion not officially blessed by its own dubious sanction. All I ask, is that careful literary pilgrims with the more courteous disposition of honest enquiry may give their time to consider these valentines, taking what they find to be just, and leaving to the future any romantic assertion proving to be personally irrelevant or provocatively tangential for present debate. This is where I have arrived in my individual search for poetry at the moment. It may not be my position a decade from now, and it was certainly not my position ten years ago. Yet, it is clearly here that I stand at present, with all the questions as well as the quandaries this truly Wiccan territory entails.

I am also mindful, that Heathen valentines without context often cause religious chaos. Indeed, without decorated borders and skilfully laced boundaries, little but triviality results. One of the few pertinent lessons to be learnt from post-modern aesthetic techniques; even if it was a lesson well known to our ancestors and exemplified in the art of ages past. Back then, student rhymers ascended through the poetic ranks as they wandered between different villages to remind their kinsfolk about historically charged heroic acts, while circulating news concerning current events. The best of them secured positions performing at an aristocrat's house, thereafter being richly rewarded for their talents. It goes without saying that such increasingly complex constructions demanded a powerful memory, and in the course of time various mnemonic devices emerged as memory aids. Embracing this innovation, the rhymers themselves realised that the pristine beauty of their compositions was verbally raised to unexpected heights. These linguistic mechanisms were, therefore, eventually built into the verses themselves. The rhymers were slowly becoming true poets.

This is why the 'oral origination' thesis of poetic composition needs to be re-examined. Every now and again, the argument asserts, someone will speak with a natural lyricism. Maybe it only happens when a person is under pressure, or intoxicated, or suddenly inspired by the tragic significance of a single event. In the final analysis however, these contingencies don't matter as much as the fact that there is a strange power in such obviously oracular utterances. They are quite literally moments of Truth, or Prophetic Occasions when we see into the fathomless heart of PSYCHE Herself; being temporarily caught between the Everything and the All in a life made more aware that sexual relationships embody Her beauty. Although impaling such moments as these into spoken text became the curse, as well as the blessing, of the rhymers.

Moreover, we are still surrounded by analogous instances of foetal wordplay on a daily basis, which either give us an insight into an individual's character or reveal a previously hidden aesthetic value. It should thus come as no surprise that a peculiar authority is rightly attributed to this uniquely human gift. A type of status recognised as Holy, Holy, Holy, by our forefathers, but usually seen as frightening or merely a question of good education by ourselves. After all, most modern rhymers are introduced to poetry as a series of carefully organised lines on a blank page, or as memorised phrases performed for a 'reading'. As such, contemporary rhymers are largely unaware that these Magical Moments transfigured the world of our ancestors, allowing them to find their rightful place in an ageless Spirit-Circle, as conquerors, farmers and composers.

On that blissful note, we still need to be careful, because even when the rhymers had become poets, they then still had to fight their way to PSYCHE'S Temple; a strange cubic building on the inner planes, honouring perfected sexual desires. Once there, its north wall is found to be an erection of Everlasting Oaths, whereas the south wall is buttressed by Broken Hearts. Most realised the east wall is an electrification of Glazed Eyes, while the west wall streams with Torrential Tears. Curiously, the ceiling and floor are constructed from Hoarfrost, marking the beginning and end of most romances. Yet in the epicentre of a building where even Theodicies are possible, Magnificent PSYCHE Herself stands immobile and dreaming about the restoration of unconditional Love through sex. Mia Culpa, my brothers and Sisters. Mia Maxima Culpa. I admit my moral error, because She has taught me that sexual love will eventually touch Purest, Purest, Spirit. An experience each valentine must undergo for themselves, before returning to the empirical spheres.

In this Radical way a small, but eroticised band of highly literate witches can, at long last, re-emerge into public view, protected by the Hallowed-Sanctity-Of-Tradition, and the Deep-Initiatory-Knowledge that female metaphors are more appropriate when trying to frame questions about Divine Realties. At that point we will no longer be homo viator, but have found our poetic path home. And I, as Her priest, already realise it as my duty to encourage participation in these Iconic Experiences by the spiritually malnourished. As Englishmen, we must once again allow poetry to define the Identity of our own ethnic community. Yes, the study and interpretation of these skin-tight documents must remain in Heathen hands alone. Only then can our Meta-Languages weave new sources of Belonging; my Dearly Beloved. And as I have now joined such rarefied ranks, finding thereby freedom in perfect service, while remaining Caliban in Clover; may I finally testify that . . .

I am lying on the ground because I am Caliban

Because I am Caliban, I am drunk

Drunk with the wine of a hidden Godhead

A wine bibber with an upturned bowl

Upturned but still to be replenished

Replenished by the blessings of the Saints.

I am lying on the ground because I am short

Short and dressed in a gown of grey

A gown that hides a Poets Gospel

Gospel news given by a hunted Fox

Hunted, yet unafraid in the knowledge

The knowledge that an Angel is ascending

I am lying on the ground because of a Giant

A Giant of fire who sits on a throne

This throne reveals His authority Divine

Authority given to a Celestial Spirit

Celestial and not from the solid world

Solid like a chalice crossed in suffering

I am lying on the ground because I am hungry

Hungry although everyday I am fed

Fed by a fish that appears in a pond

A pond like Bethesda inspired by a breath

The breath of a promise bringing health in it's quenching

Promise and fulfilment beyond any expectation.

I am lying on the ground because I am praying

Praying to the Stars for their singular kindness

A kindness that allowed the love born of ashes

Ashes whose embers light better roads to travel

Light and enlighten the tongue and the spine

The spine of a man seeking Wisdom in words.

To Austin Spare;

Under a Moon blessed thicket, regal Roebucks

Licked your lustful eyes to cleanse your vision,

To allow you to see

And observe, Christian men at war

With their Heathen hearts

My Poetic Prince of Walworth daffodils,

Silver elves,

Grey stone Boxers and Saxon chapels,

Sinister druids as retired language scholars,

Muscled ironmongers in gilded choirs,

Damp, dull, days and depressing cul-de-sacs

Fucked-up farriers committing

Facile sins,

Enflamed by unrequited temptations

Masked as wilful ineptitude.

In an isolated Court of Gothar

Between premature or derelict dimensions.

To Raymond Tallis;

With courageously cleft poems pointing

Like the devil's foot

From semantic incisions

To a philosophical Magnus Ars,

I marvelled at your momentary

Yet anxious numinosity.

Wondering when your remedial words

Would ever find my covenstead

And their wounded wings touch us

In stanzas as English as a frosty dawn

And with visions both freezing and free

Woven from fertile graveyards

To a suggestive canopy of coastal Conifers

Yielding Wisdom through pensive seasons.

To Algernon Charles Swinburne;

When did Damselflies first dance at dusk

Like electrical fairies around an ice cream cone

Ever circling your eye with radiant enquiries;

Raised as objections to the microscopes Empire?

Since you knew Art has nothing to do

With a willing suspension of disbelief

But was more closely akin

To a conscious absorption

Into the ever Creative Ideal

Although afeared that the industrial

Arms of Pluto's night

Stifle our Country with cold

Caresses, until a Saxon consciousness

Burns the Sun Himself

Through unequalled terror for intrepid

Generations as Truth becomes Beauty

Then a Reconstallating Goodness.

To Edward Dorn;

Deciphering your death

One dull, but modern afternoon,

My pulse suddenly grieved

At the passing of an era.

To The Pilgrim;

He stood by St. George against national Dragons

Despite false liberal fairies feeding vanities fair .
Tainting traditions more moderate milk.

Despite despondent Princes of ancestral essence
Abandoning both our hearts and heritage.

Despite Ogre Two-Horn named Tony-Bush
Disguised as a Dove without guile.

Despite Giant injustice waving Whitehalls gavel
Proving quite capable of silencing critics.

Despite Old Gnome Sterling's parasitic perspective
Poisoning wisdom's ever-generous marrow.

Despite vulgar binge Damsels that curse every city
Slowly enslaving each besieged weekend.

He still stands by St, George against Dragons.

To Wendy Cope; Carol Anne Duffy and Amy Winehouse, along with all those gifted women who helped me to see the world differently and were . . .

Stood on the shores of their own sea-change

Like a flock of white Tundra swans

Singing the icy British blues

On the wrong coastline

At sundown,

Provoking alchemical rats

With the method of grammar

And the aim of poetic transcendence;

Yet reminding my pen that all writing

Is either Architypal Prayer

Or pointless scribble. Oh,

Oh, Oh, those Soror Mysticas

Their Wasted lands

Are so wantonly carnivorous.

To D. Jonathan Jones;

Spirits engineer English space

With pure cascading waters

And ancient juggernauting ice

To move pollen drenched soils

Across emerald pallets fit for blessing.

Although so cold is this chill night,

You sing life's own song

As salt against snow

Warming our mechanised blood

Into a Greater Becoming.

Like a Reed Warbler on a Reed bed

Adding voice to the euphoric chorus

At the rising of bashful Ramsons,

As authentic as the day is long,

Marking the end of winters melt.

To Aleister Crowley;

Like the cock's egg

Of thieves cant

Your rhyming slang

Spoke in miracles.

To Blake's Resurgence;

His skin was the song of a wanderer's love

Calling to the Silence and the Angels

Like a pioneer retrospectively yearning

For immortal meditations beyond all sense perception,

Beyond canvassed frontiers, beyond clouded finitude,

Beyond every known bruise or embrace.

Yet skin unfolded his soul to manifest mystery;

Of floral monads swaying by his sparkling pond

With Bees bumbling in noon-tide heat over lemonade

Twists

And Dragonflies hovering over full books of folklore

By cut cucumber sandwiches on The Sunday Times News.

Of Sparrow songs echoing England's own chorus

Along leafy Oak lanes; ever framing thatched houses

Near pastured Cows between ancient Abbey ruins

Where forgotten Orchards catch transcendent light.

Of Midsummer bonfires; of market town fayres

Within which his ideal, like that of any Lover,

Made music by meadows after dancing till dawn

Almost chivalrous towards his fleshly refrain

As a bone harp played by Christ's fingers.

Selective Glossary

Alchemy: A literary genre, developed though the millenia by empirically minded symbolists such as Newton and Jung to codify the analogical associations surrounding sacred oils, astrologically aligned minerals and medicinal unctions, all of which were used to quicken inner explorations. It is something of a misnomer to state that alchemy was simply a primitive form of chemistry, since these gifted scholars specifically created a cross-cultural Imagistic vocabulary in order to discuss highly abstract metaphysical issues without the doctrinal limitations usually associated with organised religions.

Asgarth: An Anglo-Saxon spelling for the city of the God's, or in other words the totality of Eternal Self. Post-modern theoreticians often describe this Kingdom of the Cosmic Mind as a rarified level of consciousness wherein a poet discovers his or her Immortal Literary essence amongst the Spirits of Light and Sound.

Athame: The will of a witch in the para-physical shape of a ceremonial dagger or rebellious nib. Unlike the quill characteristic of a playwright, this arcane instrument intensifies and manipulates the feeling of a place through its use in ritual, either at a psychologically significant location or on paper.

Grimoire; Although the French word for grammatology, it is also a book detailing the textual methods of notation by which the great northern scholar Saxo Grammaticus initially developed his semantics of Witchcraft. These days, such Imagist volumes usually take the form of black and white vellum manuals, and are occasionally used for ethno-ritual purposes.

Imaginal: A word apparently coined by the French Scholar Henri Corbin to describe the psycho-objective reality between Myth and Symbol.

Incantations: At one level the growling, grunting and systematised screaming employed by a witch to reach more deeply into the sub-conscious mind so as to unleash its primordial powers. Conversely, the sophisticated and deeply erotic stanzas used to induce purely aesthetic states of consciousness.

Initiation: An expansion of personal Imagist consciousness as the poet takes a pivotal step towards atavistic fulfilment.

Ostara: It is difficult to discern whether the name of our Goddess as recorded by Roman writers reflects the original form of this formula, or if modern re-constructions such as Oestra have solved this mythic mystery. After all, the name of a Goddess or God in Heathenism reflects a view of life governed by a celestial intelligence in the other world.

Poetry: The act of beautifying conversation and prose through the use of imagery and rhythm to enrich communication. It is consequently the highest literary process, historically adept at using lexical items to unlock the doors of textual cognition in order to expose the realities of the world in depth. Derrida is indeed correct in pointing out that originally there was a cultural resistance to writing iconic stanzas down on papyrus, due to the perceived sanctity of living, oral, Imagism.

Transcendent Principle: The hylozoistic assertion that everything is always more than the number of its beastial bones and a fact of healthy, common, experience.

Wicca; An Old English abstract noun for Heavenly wisdom or practical knowledge, largely misapplied as a term in modern times since it now largely refers to a contemporary religious ideology closely allied to the Feminist Movement. This diminution of meaning is the reason why present day Heathens tend to feel uncomfortable with its general usage. After all, Anglo-Saxon Witchcraft was not clearly distinct from other branches of learning

Grammar of Witchcraft 91

www.ingramcontent.com/pod-product-compliance
Lightning Source LLC
Chambersburg PA
CBHW070937160426
43193CB00011B/1717